PEOPLE POWER

Peaceful Protests That Changed the World

Rebecca June Ximo Abadía

Translated by José Enrique Macián

PRESTEL
Munich · London · New York

People Power

Sometimes, when we are faced with an injustice, it may seem too hard to take action. It feels easier just to sit at home and do nothing. But often, doing nothing only leads to more disappointment and frustration. A feeling of helplessness takes hold of us.

Laying out a plan of action and insisting that our voices be heard—in a peaceful but forceful way—will make you feel better, even if, in the end, you don't achieve everything you'd hoped for. Work together. Share your hopes and worries for the future with others. This is the most powerful magic there is.

In this book, you will learn how peaceful protests have made a difference around the world—from India to New Zealand, from the United Kingdom to Estonia—and discover that when people come together to protest peacefully, they become extremely powerful. For generations, peaceful demands have served to bring about social change, draw attention to special causes, and defend human rights. When a group of courageous people stands up for what they believe, amazing things can happen! The stories in this book will convince you that the most powerful magic of all is the power of the people.

The Mud March (United Kingdom, 1907)
Up to their knees in mud for the right to vote

Gandhi's Salt March (India, 1930)
The fistful of salt that drove the British from India

The Montgomery Bus Boycott (United States, 1955)
The day Rosa Parks said, "No!"

The Defenders of Pureora Forest (New Zealand, 1978)
To save the forest, they climbed its ancient trees

The Greenham Common Women's Peace Camp (United Kingdom, 1982)
The activists who surrounded a nuclear base

The People Power Revolution (Philippines, 1986)
The victory of Filipinos against the Marcos dictatorship

The Singing Revolution (Estonia, 1988)
One hundred thousand voices rang out for Estonian independence

The Fall of the Berlin Wall (Germany, 1989)
"We are the people"—the cry that brought down the Wall

The March for Territory and Dignity (Bolivia, 1990)
The voice of Indigenous peoples echoed throughout Bolivia

Women of Liberia Mass Action for Peace (Liberia, 2003)
Liberian women marched for the end of civil war

The Jasmine Revolution (Tunisia, 2011)
The Tunisian wave of anti-authoritarian protest became a tsunami

Fridays for Future (Sweden/Global, 2019)
When Greta dared to stand up for the planet in need

Black Lives Matter (United States/Global, 2020)
Millions of people continue to demand racial justice around the world

The Mud March

Like in most of the world, when democracy began to take off in the United Kingdom, women could neither vote in elections nor participate in making political decisions. Many worried that if women were allowed to vote, they would be too busy outside the home and start to neglect their housework and taking care of the children.

Then, in the early twentieth century, British women became increasingly active in politics. They organized themselves into groups and campaigned to demand suffrage: the right to vote.

At the time, though some men supported their cause, the majority of politicians (all of whom were men) did not approve of women being allowed to vote.

On a rainy, wintry day in 1907, thousands of women filled the streets of London, chanting, "Votes for women!" They did not care that their boots and skirts became covered in mud as they walked, because the reason behind their protest was far more important. They marched from Hyde Park to the Strand, through the heart of the city. The protest became known as the Mud March. Women from different backgrounds and social classes participated, demonstrating the broad support for their cause. It was the largest protest to date demanding the right to vote for women.

Women in the United Kingdom finally gained the right to vote in 1928, after more than half a century of activism.

Gandhi's Salt March

In 1930, in India, the population was tired of being ruled by British colonizers. Indian men and women felt that they were treated unfairly under the colonial regime. They wanted to be governed by their own people and put an end to the British exploitation of their country's natural resources. They were fed up with the regulations that oppressed them, such as the Salt Laws which prohibited them from collecting or selling this important mineral. Salt had become so expensive that the majority of Indians could no longer afford to buy it.

Dressed in traditional Indian clothing, Mahatma Gandhi
and his followers decided to walk 240 miles to
a coastal salt mine in protest against the Salt Laws.
As they marched, many other Indians identified with their
cause and joined the group. This large crowd of people
walked peacefully through the open fields of India
for twenty-four days. When they finally arrived
at the mine, Gandhi picked up a handful of natural salt
from the ground in defiance of the law.

Many other Indians followed suit and staged similar
mass protests at salt mines across the country.
In this way, a campaign of civil disobedience began
against British rule that opened the door to
India's independence in 1947.

The Montgomery Bus Boycott

For many years in the United States, racial segregation meant that Black people were denied free use of public spaces. They ate at different restaurants from white people, went to different schools, stores, and libraries, and were even buried in different cemeteries. Those with dark skin were treated as inferior and had fewer rights in the eyes of the law.

On public buses, Black passengers had to give up certain seats to their fellow white passengers. One day in 1955, in Montgomery, Alabama, an African American woman named Rosa Parks was riding the bus home from work when a white man got on and the driver demanded that she give up her seat. Bravely, she refused. The police arrested and fined her.

In response to this injustice, the Black population of Montgomery organized a boycott of the city buses, known as the Montgomery Bus Boycott. On the first day, forty thousand citizens refused to get on the buses. Instead of taking public transportation, they walked or carpooled, and Black taxi drivers reduced their fares for them. The boycott lasted a whole year, until finally the city changed the rules of racial segregation on buses.

This was one of the first mass protests demanding fair treatment for African Americans. It led to hundreds more protests, which managed over time to change unjust laws that differentiated people based on the color of their skin.

The Defenders of Pureora Forest

New Zealand is a country made up of several islands in the Pacific Ocean. It was one of the last habitable landmasses to be populated by humans. The Māori, originally from Polynesia, were the first to settle on these islands, after which 80% of the New Zealand territory was still covered in forests. When European settlers arrived, however, they began to build houses in an unsustainable way, cutting down more and more trees to convert into boards. Logging destroyed many of New Zealand's native forests.

Pureora Forest is a tropical rainforest located on the North Island of New Zealand, and it is an important site in Māori culture. In 1978, deforestation and logging began in this forest, home to a huge variety of wild animals and plants, including the oldest evergreen trees from the genus *Podocarpus* in the world. Some specimens are over a thousand years old.

Local environmental activists wanted to save Pureora Forest. They knew that deforestation would endanger the wildlife and ancient trees. So, they decided to take action against it. They snuck into the forest, climbed several trees, built platforms there, and refused to come down. They knew that the loggers wouldn't be able to cut down the trees if they were in the way.

Sure enough, the loggers had to stop and were furious, while the protest drew the attention of the news media and all New Zealanders.

Thanks to the activists, Pureora Forest was saved. Today it is an important site for both tourism and ecological study. As a result of the protest, the New Zealand Government ended the felling of all native forests that were owned by the state.

The Greenham Common Women's Peace Camp

Nuclear weapons are weapons of mass destruction: explosive devices that can destroy entire cities, with devastating effects on humanity, wildlife, and nature.

In 1981, the Government of the United Kingdom decided to allow the United States to store ninety-six nuclear cruise missiles at Greenham Common, a small American air base in the English countryside.

A courageous group of women from Wales decided to take action
against this decision. They set out on a ten-day trek to the Greenham
Common military base, where they set up camp. Thirty-six women
of different ages and social backgrounds led the march.
They didn't want to lose their husbands and sons to another war.
They wanted to put an end to the violence.

News of their protest spread across the country, and on December 12, 1982, thirty thousand protesters rallied together to surround the site under the slogan "Embrace the Base!" News of the protest reached the ears of many people across the United Kingdom and the world.

The Greenham Common Women's Peace Camp remained active for many years. The removal of nuclear weapons from the base was completed in 1991, but the peace activists continued their anti-nuclear protest until 2000.

The People Power Revolution

Ferdinand Marcos was elected president of the Philippines in 1965 and again in 1969. As time passed, Filipinos felt increasingly helpless under his government. The gap between rich and poor—who made up the majority of the population—kept growing.

In 1972, President Marcos declared martial law, with which he granted himself special powers, including control of the armed forces and the power to limit freedom of speech, freedom of the press, and other civil liberties. Later, he arrested all his opponents and, because of that, was able to stay in power for another fourteen years.

After many years of discontent, the people of the Philippines decided to take action and voice their unhappiness at the way their country was being governed. On February 23, 1986, a major avenue called Epifanio de los Santos in Manila, the capital of the Philippines, began to fill with people. Little by little, more and more people heard about the protest—by word of mouth or on the radio—and joined the demonstration.

Before long, more than two million unarmed civilians had gathered along the avenue. Despite the seriousness of the situation, the atmosphere on the street was joyful, like a gigantic block party. After three days, Marcos had to accept defeat and flee the country.

The Singing Revolution

Estonia, a small country in northeastern Europe, has always had a special relationship with music. Traditional folk songs are an important part of Estonian culture and help Estonians feel connected to their country, language, and identity.

Previously governed by different countries of the Baltic region, the Estonian people fought hard for their independence and obtained it in 1918. But in 1939, Estonia was invaded by the Soviet Union under Joseph Stalin. Many people fled the country while others were expelled.

Despite attempts by the Soviet government to impose their own culture and customs, Estonians continued to perform their folk songs and traditional music to keep their culture alive. They carried on singing together and celebrating festivals such as Laulupidu, the Estonian Song Festival, which takes place every five years. The powerful sound of their voices singing together rekindled their faith in themselves. It reminded them of their strength and showed them that they were not alone in their desire for independence.

In 1988, approximately one hundred thousand Estonians gathered at the grounds of the Estonian Song Festival in Tallinn, the country's capital, to sing together for five nights in a row. Estonian flags were soon unfurled as those present chanted, "I am Estonian and I will remain Estonian." These peaceful acts demonstrated the strength and determination of the Estonian people and contributed to their regaining independence in 1990.

The Fall of the Berlin Wall

Can you imagine what it would be like if a wall were built in the middle of your city or town so that you couldn't visit the other side? That's just what happened in Berlin in 1961, at a time when Germany was divided in two, between East and West. The East German government built a wall to prevent people in the East from fleeing to the West, where there were more freedoms and better job opportunities. The wall cut the city of Berlin into two halves, separating families and friends. It was over three meters high and guarded by soldiers.

In West Berlin, the wall was covered in colorful graffiti. But in East Berlin, where freedom of speech and expression was limited, the wall was gray.

Every Monday, in the church of St. Nicholas in the city of Leipzig, in East Germany, a small group of people began to organize peaceful prayer vigils asking for liberty and justice. Although they were very scared—they didn't know how the government would react—more and more people joined these meetings every week. Realizing that they were not alone gave them courage, and as the movement grew, the protesters became even more daring. They took their protest from the church to the streets.

During the night of October 9, 1989, seventy thousand people participated in a protest in Leipzig. They carried lighted candles and chanted "We are the people!" Although acts of protest were against the law, the authorities did not respond with violence, so other similar protests began to spread throughout East Germany. These demonstrations led to the fall of the Berlin Wall on November 9, 1989, when the government in the East was forced to allow people to pass over into the West. The Wall was dismantled in 1990.

The March for Territory and Dignity

In Bolivia, Indigenous peoples have been living on their lands for thousands of years and make up a large part of the population. There are thirty-six recognized native groups in the country, including the Aymara, Quechua, Chiquitano, Guaraní, Mojeños, Sirionó, and Tsimané.

However, the Indigenous way of life is in constant danger due to deforestation, the invasion of settlers, and the exploitation of natural resources. In 1990, Indigenous peoples living in the Bolivian lowlands felt seriously threatened by non-Indigenous ranchers, loggers, and farmers destroying Native territories.

On August 15, 1990, three hundred Indigenous people from the lowlands of Bolivia set out on the March for Territory and Dignity. Enduring torrential rains, mud, and intense sun, they walked from Trinidad, capital of the department of Beni, through the Amazon basin and the high plateau of the Altiplano, until they reached La Paz, the capital of Bolivia. Every step they took was a symbol of their determination to protect their ancestral way of life. Other Indigenous peoples joined them in the march, and by the time they reached their destination, there were more than eight hundred protestors.

In La Paz, they demanded a meeting with the government of President Jaime Paz Zamora. Their courageous march led the state to officially recognize the existence of these Indigenous peoples as distinct groups, as well as their collective ownership of certain areas of land. It was a historic achievement for the Indigenous populations of Latin America.

Women of Liberia Mass Action for Peace

For many years, Liberia was a country divided by conflict. Violence was part of daily life for Liberians, and the ethnic group you belonged to determined how you were treated. In 2003, the country had been immersed in a civil war for fourteen years.

Many people had been driven from their homes and many others had been killed. Men and boys were forced to become soldiers—or else threatened with violence—and some women even tried to hide their husbands and sons to keep them safe.

Unwilling to tolerate the war any longer, a group of Liberian women decided it was up to them to take matters into their own hands and end the conflict. They had suffered in silence long enough and could no longer take it. It was time to say no to violence and yes to peace.

Dressed all in white to symbolize peace, hundreds of women began to gather daily at the fish market in the capital, Monrovia. They sang and prayed together to demand an end to the civil war. They managed to force a meeting with the Liberian president, Charles Taylor, and made him promise that he would participate in peace talks.

Later, they went to the Executive Mansion, the residence of the President where negotiations were taking place, and staged a silent sit-in. They blocked all doors and windows and prevented the negotiators from leaving the peace talks without a resolution.

Their actions ended fourteen years of civil war and brought peace to Liberia. These events also inspired Liberian women to become more active in politics, resulting in the election of Africa's first female head of state: Ellen Johnson Sirleaf.

The Jasmine Revolution

In 2011, President Zine al-Abidine Ben Ali had ruled Tunisia for twenty-three years, and many people felt that a change was needed. The government had grown increasingly repressive and freedom of speech was limited. The Tunisian people wanted more liberties and to hold elections for a new leader.

Despite various initiatives to reduce poverty, life in Tunisia was difficult for most of its inhabitants, particularly those who lived in cities. They struggled to survive due to lack of work, rising food prices, and poor living conditions.

In December 2010, fed up with his inability to make a living and support his family, Mohamed Bouazizi set himself on fire in front of the regional governor's office. The desperate act of this street vendor provoked mass demonstrations in Sidi Bouzid, a city in central Tunisia. News of the protests spread across the country and the anger and frustration that many people had suppressed for years pushed them into the streets. The demonstrators chanted, "Bread, freedom, and social dignity." Thousands of people were united by their desire for a free and just Tunisia.

These were the largest protests that Tunisia had experienced in many years. They lasted twenty-eight days, until President Ben Ali left power and fled the country with his family. Information about the events in Tunisia reached everywhere and inspired similar protests in several nearby countries, a movement which would become known as the Arab Spring.

Fridays for Future

Scientists have been warning about climate change for decades, and every year there is more evidence that pollution and the use of fossil fuels are having damaging effects on our planet.

The effects of climate change are evident and continue to increase.
But very few adults seem to take it seriously, particularly those in power.
Young people all over the world, however, are concerned. They question,
why aren't governments doing more to combat climate change?

When news broke in 2019 that 15-year-old Greta Thunberg was staging a climate protest on the steps of the Swedish Parliament in her hometown of Stockholm, her actions immediately galvanized young people around the world to also stand up.

SAVE OUR

Soon, a new movement was born: Fridays for Future (FFF).

Not yet able to vote or participate in the major decisions that would affect their future, teenagers and children across the globe began using the only tool they had at hand: regular peaceful protests. Now, around the world, Friday has become a day of school strikes and street protests. Students continue to demand that governments take urgent and immediate action to prevent further climate change, including banning the use of fossil fuels. Young people are finding a way to make their voices heard.

Black Lives Matter

Black people around the world continue to be discriminated against simply because of the color of their skin. In the United States, African Americans are three times more likely than white people to be killed by the police.

When this happens and those responsible for the deaths are not charged, it sends the message that the lives of Black people do not matter, that they don't have the same value as those of other people.

In 2020, after a police officer unlawfully and ruthlessly killed an African American man named George Floyd, people across the globe, but especially in the United States, took to the streets to express their outrage and to deliver an important message: Black Lives Matter. The voices of the protesters resounded around the world, and more and more people have since joined the protest movement.

These peaceful demands demonstrate widespread support for police reform in the United States. Through the protestors' call for an end to police brutality and racial injustice, people across the globe have been made aware of the violence and discrimination still faced by Black people in the United States and in other parts of the world. Much remains to be done, but the powerful message of the Black Lives Matter (BLM) movement has changed our world and society forever.

For Darío.
Ximo Abadía

To Mia and Adele, for inspiring me.

To Alex, for believing in me.

To Hugh, Kiki, and Gilly, for teaching me
how to fight injustice.
Rebecca June

© for the Spanish edition: 2022, Zahorí Books under the title:
People Power. Protestas que han cambiado el mundo
© for the English edition: 2023, Prestel Verlag, Munich · London · New York
A member of Penguin Random House Verlagsgruppe GmbH
Neumarkter Strasse 28 · 81673 Munich
© text: 2022, Rebecca June
© illustrations: 2022, Ximo Abadía

Library of Congress Control Number: 2022944135
A CIP catalogue record for this book is available from the British Library.

Translated from the Spanish by José Enrique Macián

Project management: Constanze Holler
Copyediting: Ayesha Wadhawan
Production management: Susanne Hermann
Printing and binding: Índice Artes gráficas, Barcelona

Prestel Publishing compensates the CO_2 emissions produced from
the making of this book by supporting a reforestation project in Brazil.
Find further information on the project here:
www.ClimatePartner.com/14044-1912-1001

Penguin Random House Verlagsgruppe FSC® N001967
ISBN 978-3-7913-7540-3